Q and A

The little book of questions on....

COCKTAILS

Copyright © 2013 Two Magpies Publishing
An imprint of Read Publishing Ltd
Home Farm, 44 Evesham Road, Cookhill, Alcester,
Warwickshire, B49 5LJ

Commissioning Editor Rose Hewlett
Words by Sophie Berry
Design and Illustrations by Zoë Horn Haywood

This book is copyright and may not be reproduced or copied in any way without the express permission of the publisher in writing.

British Library Cataloguing-in-Publication Data A catalogue record for this book is available from the British Library.

CONTENTS

Introduction 3

History 7

Equipment 13

Preparation 21

Recipes 29

Top Tips and Tricks 68

INTRODUCTION

MAKING COCKTAILS AT HOME IS A WONDERFUL PASTIME!

Making cocktails at home is a wonderful pastime. Learning how to mix and blend to make original and delicious beverages is a fun past time which will make parties and special occasions that bit more special.

Added to this, you can make them exactly how you like, adding your favourite ingredients to make a perfect, personalised drink.

Hopefully you are now feeling inspired to get started on your first recipe. This little book will endeavour to answer any questions you have about the cocktail-making process, from what equipment you'll need to find, to what kind of glass to serve your carefully-created cocktails in.

ALL THAT'S LEFT TO SAY IS -
GOOD LUCK!

HISTORY

Q. What is a cocktail?

A. A cocktail is an alcoholic drink, comprising mixed and blended spirits. A cocktail usually consists of three or more ingredients.

Q. Where does the word 'cocktail' come from?

A. Some people believe the word cocktail is used to describe a mixed drink, as the term is also used to refer to a mixed-breed horse. In the past, a mixed-breed horse would have its tail cut short, to identify it. These horses were called 'cocktails', and it is believed the name was adopted to describe a mixed beverage.

Q. How long has the word 'cocktail' been used to describe a mixed drink?

A. The origin of the word 'cocktail' is often disputed, although many believe the first recorded use of the word cocktail to be from The Morning Post and Gazetteer in London, England in 1798. Before this mention was discovered, the earliest-known use of the word in print was from 1806, and found in an upstate New York newspaper.

EQUIPMENT

Q. What do I need to source before making my own cocktails?

A. You will need to source a good cocktail shaker, mixing glass, barspoon and strainer.

Q. Is that it? Many recipes ask for crushed ice, how do I go about this?

A. You may also need a blender, or ice crusher. You can crush ice by hand, too. Simply wrap the cubes in a clean cloth and bash them against a hard surface to break the ice into smaller pieces.

Q. What about decoration, drink accessories and garnishes?

A. Try and source some straws and stirrers. You will also need a sharp knife for slicing fruit and peel for garnishing.

Q. What kind of glasses will I need?

A. Sourcing the right glasses for each cocktail you make will really add to the aesthetic appeal of your creations, and give your drinks an authentic look.

Q. How many different types of glass are there?

A. There are many different types of glass, but the main four you will need are Martini glasses, Champagne flutes, highball glasses and Old Fashioned glasses.

Q. What do these glasses look like?

A. The traditional Martini glass is a triangle shaped glass with a delicate, long stem. A flute is the the type of glass you serve Champagne in, and has a slim glass and a delicate, long stem. An Old Fashioned glass is a short and sturdy tumbler, and a highball glass is a tall glass, and often slimmer at the bottom than the top.

Q. What is a base spirit?

A. A base spirit is the alcohol that will make up the base of your cocktail, eg. vodka.

Q. What kind of alcohol do I need to use as a base spirit?

A. Recipes will call for all different base spirits. However, vodka, rum gin and whisky are all popular base spirits.

Q. Do you have to mix all cocktails in a cocktail shaker?

A. No, there are numerous mixing methods, however, a cocktail shaker is most commonly used.

Q. What other ways can you mix cocktails?

A. You can mix some cocktails in a mixing glass, using a barspoon. This is known as muddling.

Q. How do you know whether to shake or stir?

A. A general rule of thumb is to shake cocktails which include fruit juices, cream liqueurs, syrup, eggs, or dairy products. All others should be stirred.

Q. Does it make a difference whether you shake or stir?

A. Stirring is a more gentle technique for mixing cocktails and is a delicate way of combining flavours and ingredients. Many gin-based cocktails, such as Martinis, use this technique so as not to 'bruise the gin'.

Q. What is a really simple cocktail recipe I can start off with?

A. Why not try a Harvey Wallbanger? This cocktail appeared during a new wave of cocktails in the 1970s. Simply comprising vodka, Galliano, and orange juice, Harvey Wallbangers are a household favourite, and still enjoyed widely today.

HARVEY WALLBANGER

INGREDIENTS

1 part vodka
3 parts orange juice
3 dashes Galliano

METHOD

1. In a cocktail shaker, mix the vodka and the orange juice.
2. Pour into an ice-filled highball glass.
3. Add the dashes of Galliano before serving.

Q. James Bond drinks Martinis. Can I make these at home?

A. Over the years, and with the help of the James Bond character, the Martini has become one of the best-known mixed alcoholic beverages. Bond prefers his Martinis shaken but W. Somerset Maugham declared that "Martinis should always be stirred, not shaken, so that the molecules lie sensuously, one on top of the other." Try this classic recipe for a dry Martini.

DRY MARTINI

INGREDIENTS

5 parts gin
1 part dry vermouth
Twist of lemon, to garnish

METHOD

1. Place the chilled ingredients in a Martini glass.
2. Serve with a twist of lemon.

Q. Is there a recipe I can try at home for a Martini which isn't the classic gin recipe?

A. Here is a great recipe for Vodkatinis. This cocktail is perfect for vodka-lovers, and you can really get creative with the garnishes that you add. Try a small silverskin onion, or a cocktail olive for a savoury, salty finish to your drink.

VODKATINI

INGREDIENTS

5 parts vodka
1 part dry vermouth
Twist of lemon, to garnish

METHOD

1. In an ice-filled cocktail shaker mix the ingredients.
2. Pour through a strainer into a chilled Martini glass.
3. Add a twist of lemon before serving.

Q. Is there a good cocktail recipe I can try for a drink I can serve before a meal?

A. Made with tomato juice, vodka, and array of tangy, spicy additions, a Bloody Mary is the perfect way to start a meal.

BLOODY MARY

INGREDIENTS

1 part vodka
4 parts tomato juice
1 dash lemon juice
2 dashes Worcestershire sauce
1 pinch celery salt
Tabasco sauce, to taste
Pepper, to taste

METHOD

1. In a cocktail shaker, mix all of the ingredients except the Tabasco sauce and pepper.
2. Pour over ice in a goblet.
3. Add Tabasco sauce and pepper to taste, and serve.

Q. I'd like to make a short, simple cocktail to serve as an aperitif which isn't as spicy as a Bloody Mary! What is a good recipe to try?

A. A French Connection is a delicious cocktail made with Cognac and amaretto. Served in an 'Old Fashioned' glass, a French Connection is a short, strong drink which is perfect as an aperitif.

FRENCH CONNECTION

INGREDIENTS

1 part brandy
1 part amaretto

METHOD

1. In a cocktail shaker, mix the brandy and amaretto.
2. Pour into an ice-filled tumbler.

Q. What is a good cocktail to serve after dinner?

A. Why not try an Espresso Martini? This cocktail is the perfect alternative to an after-dinner coffee.

ESPRESSO MARTINI

INGREDIENTS

2 parts vodka
1 part Khalúa
3 parts coffee

METHOD

1. In an ice-filled cocktail shaker, mix the ingredients well.
2. Pour through a strainer into a chilled Martini glass.
3. Garnish with coffee beans before serving.

Q. What is a simple and straightforward cocktail to make with Champagne?

A. A Kir Royale is the perfect drink to make with Champagne. You can substitute the Champagne for white wine if you wish, and make a slightly different beverage. A Kir Royale made with white wine is simply called a Kir.

KIR ROYALE

INGREDIENTS

1 glass chilled Champagne
2 dashes creme de cassis

METHOD

1. Pour the chilled Champagne into a Champagne flute.
2. Add the cassis and serve.

Q. I'd love to make a rum-based cocktail, but would like to try something quite simple. What is a good recipe to start me off?

A. Try making a Dark and Stormy. It's a delicious, spicy rum-based cocktail made with dark rum and ginger beer. The Dark and Stormy is the official national drink of Bermuda, where Gosling's Black Seal Rum is made. This classic drink is popular worldwide, especially in many British Commonwealth countries, such as Australia.

DARK AND STORMY

INGREDIENTS

2 parts dark rum
4 parts ginger beer
2 lime wedges

METHOD

1. In a cocktail shaker, mix the rum and ginger beer over ice.
2. Squeeze in one of the lime wedges, and shake again.
3. Pour into a highball glass filled with crushed ice, and garnish with lime.

Q. What is another good rum-based cocktail?

A. Why not try a Zombie? This rum-based cocktail is not for the faint hearted! Using three different types of rum, this drink is strong, long, and is given a fresh kick with the mint sprig garnish.

ZOMBIE

INGREDIENTS

2 parts white rum
2 parts dark rum
2 parts golden rum
1 part apricot brandy
1 part lime juice
1 part pineapple juice
1 dash gomme syrup
1 splash Demeraran rum
Sprig of mint (for garnish)

METHOD

1. Shake all of the ingredients except the Demeraran rum and mint together in a cocktail shaker.
2. Serve in an ice-filled highball glass.
3. Splash in the Demeraran rum before serving, and garnish with a sprig of mint.

Q. I love the refreshing flavour of mint in an alcoholic beverage. Is there a simple cocktail recipe containing mint?

A. Why not try a mint julep? This cocktail is associated with the Southern states of America, being as it is based on the traditional Southern spirit, bourbon. Mint, water and sugar are added to make a refreshing drink, perfect served with the traditionally spicy foods of the South.

MINT JULEP

INGREDIENTS

6-8 leaves fresh mint
1 tbsp sugar
1 tbsp water
1 part bourbon

METHOD

1. Place 4-5 leaves in a highball glass
2. Sprinkle the sugar and water over the leaves and crush together with a barspoon until the sugar has dissolved.
3. Add the bourbon, and top up with crushed ice.
4. Garnish with the remaining mint before serving.

Q. I love Mojitos, and would like to make them at home. What is the recipe?

A. Here is a good recipe for Mojitos, the refreshing rum and mint-based Cuban cocktail.

MOJITO

INGREDIENTS

1 1/2 limes, cut into wedges
20 mint leaves
2 1/2 tsp granulated sugar
crushed ice
3 parts rum
1 part soda water

METHOD

1. Place the limes, mint and sugar into a mixing glass and 'muddle' or mash with the end of a barspoon to bruise the mint and release the lime juice.
2. Add the ice and pour over the rum.
3. Add soda water to taste and stir well. Garnish with a mint sprig and serve.

Q. What is a good bourbon-based cocktail recipe I can try?

A. Try making an Old Fashioned. The recipe was said to have been invented by a bartender at that club in honor of Colonel James E. Pepper, a prominent bourbon distiller, who brought the cocktail to the Waldorf-Astoria Hotel bar in New York City.

OLD FASHIONED

INGREDIENTS

2 parts bourbon
2 dashes Angostura bitters
1 part water
1 tsp sugar
1 orange wedge

METHOD

1. Mix the sugar, water and bitters in an Old Fashioned glass.
2. Add the orange wedge, and muddle with a barspoon.
3. Add the bourbon and a handful of ice cubes and stir before serving.

Q. I'd love to make a sweet and summery cocktail to enjoy on a sunny day. What is a good recipe to try?

A. Why not make a Piña Colada? It's a holiday favourite, and the sweetness of the pineapple is the perfect flavour for a sunny day. Try this recipe at home; it is simple, straightforward, and deliciously sweet.

PIÑA COLADA

INGREDIENTS

1 part rum
1 part Malibu
1 part coconut cream
1 part pineapple juice
3-4 pineapple chunks
Maraschino cherry, to garnish

METHOD

1. In a blender, blitz the rums, coconut cream, pineapple juice and pineapple chunks until smooth.

2. Pour into an ice-filled highball, and add a maraschino cherry to serve.

Q. What is another holiday-favourite cocktail I can try at home?

A. How about a Tequila Sunrise? Tequila Sunrise was originally served at the Arizona Biltmore Hotel, where it was created by Gene Sulit in the 1930s or 1940s. It is still widely made and enjoyed today.

TEQUILA SUNRISE

INGREDIENTS

2 parts tequila
1 part orange juice
2 dashes Grenadine

METHOD

1. In an ice-filled cocktail shaker mix the tequila and orange juice.
2. Pour into a chilled highball glass, and add the Grenadine before serving.

Q. What is another good Summer cocktail?

A. Try a Yellow Bird. Served in an icy highball glass as a lusciously long beverage it is the perfect drink for a summer's day. Experiment with garnishes for this distinctively-coloured drink, such as a wedge of lime.

YELLOW BIRD

INGREDIENTS

3 parts white rum
1 part Galliano
1 part Cointreau
1 part fresh lime juice

METHOD

1. In a cocktail shaker mix the ingredients together.
2. Pour, unstrained, into an ice-filled highball glass

Q. Is there a good recipe for a warming cocktail i can serve on a cold day?

A. Try a Rusty Nail, which is perfect for whisky lovers. Carefully scorching the lemon peel for a couple of seconds with a lit match before dropping it into your ice-filled glass will really release the zesty flavours from the rind, leaving a sharp, citrus aroma which will flavour your cocktail to perfection.

RUSTY NAIL

INGREDIENTS

2 parts Scotch whisky
1 part Drambuie
Twist of lemon peel, to garnish

METHOD

1. Stir the whisky and Drambuie together in an Old Fashioned glass with a barspoon.
2. Garnish with the lemon peel before serving.

Q. What is a good cocktail to serve at Christmas time?

A. Eggnog is traditionally enjoyed at Christmas. Using eggs in your cocktail recipes will give your drinks a distinctive taste and texture. There are a number of recipes which call for either eggs, or egg whites, but this is one of the most well known.

EGGNOG

INGREDIENTS

1 part brandy
1 part dark rum
1 egg
2 dashes gomme syrup
3 parts milk
Nutmeg, to garnish

METHOD

1. In a cocktail shaker, mix the brandy, rum, egg and syrup together.
2. Strain into a large tumbler or goblet.
3. Add the milk to the mixture in the glass, and grate a little nutmeg over to garnish.

Q. What other egg-based cocktail recipes can I try at home?

A. XYZ is another egg-based cocktail, using a hint of the distinctively-flavoured liqueur, Cointreau. If you wanted to add a garnish to this unusual beverage, a piece of orange peel, lightly scorched by a flame would complement the Cointreau perfectly.

XYZ

INGREDIENTS

2 parts rum
1 part Cointreau
1 part lemon juice
1 dash egg white

METHOD

1. In an ice-filled cocktail shaker mix the ingredients together.
2. Pour through a strainer into a chilled highball glass to serve.

Q. I'd like to make a creamy cocktail, but don't want to use egg. What is a good recipe to try?

A. Try making White Russian. White Russians are sweet and creamy cocktail and are the perfect alternative to a desert after a heavy meal.

WHITE RUSSIAN

INGREDIENTS

2 parts vodka
1 part Khalúa
2 parts milk

METHOD

1. In an ice-filled cocktail shaker mix the vodka, Khalúa and milk together.

2. Pour through a strainer into a chilled ice-filled highball glass to serve.

TOP TEN TIPS

1. Get all of your utensils and equipment ready before you start mixing your cocktails.

2. Make sure your cocktail shaker is rinsed clean after each drink is mixed.

3. Citrus fruits make a great garnish, but experiment with other fruits to decorate your carefully-created cocktails.

4. Remember to offer your guests a drink of water between each cocktail; the true alcohol content of a cocktail is often hard to gauge as the taste is masked with delicious fruit juices and mixers!

5. Try storing your glasses in a freezer before use, for a fantastic frosted finish on your glassware.

6. Hunt in charity shops and thrift stores for traditional cocktail glasses, you might get lucky and find some great pieces.

AND TRICKS

7. Substituting the alcohol in your cocktails for fruit juices and cordials is a great way to make an alcohol-free beverage that can be enjoyed by all.

8. Keep an eye out for fun stirrers and straws when you enjoy drinks at a cocktail bar. They can be recycled and used at home to give your homemade cocktails a professional touch.

9. You can get really creative and make your own home-made liqueurs to use in your cocktail making.

10. Making and designing your own cocktails is the perfect way to mark a special occasion, such as a birthday or engagement. You can even give the cocktail a special name, and make your celebration extra memorable.

NOTES

NOTES

Image Credits

All Pages - This work is a derivative of "Textures Paper IMG_0006" is Copyright ©2007-2012 ~Dioma, made available on DeviantArt under Creative Commons Attribution 2.0 Generic (CC BY 2.0) http//dioma.deviantart.com/art/Textures-Paper-58028330

All Pages - This work is a derivative of "Textures Paper IMG_0002" is Copyright ©2007-2012 Dioma, made available on DeviantArt under Creative Commons Attribution 2.0 Generic (CC BY 2.0) http//dioma.deviantart.com/art/Textures-Paper-58028330

All Chapter Pages - This work is a derivative of "Frame back" is copyright © 2009 Sunset Sailor made available on Flickr under Creative Commons Attribution 2.0 Generic (CC BY 2.0) http://www.flickr.com/photos/sunsetsailor/3558408492

Pages 2-3 - This work is a derivative of "Hawaiin Cocktails" is copyright © 2012 By Taz, Sporkist, made available on Flickr under Creative Commons Attribution 2.0 Generic (CC BY 2.0) http://www.flickr.com/photos/sporkist/6879316765/

Pages 6-7 - This work is a derivative of "Rum, Manhattan, Tequila Old Fashioned.jpg" is copyright © 2012 By Marler, made available on Wikimedia Commons, Attribution-ShareAlike 3.0 Unported (CC BY-SA 3.0), http://commons.wikimedia.org/wiki/File%3ARum%2C_Manhattan%2C_Tequila_Old_Fashioned.jpg

Page 11 - This work is a derivative of "Jerry Slater's Bufala Negra cocktail" is copyright ©2008 Southern Foodways Alliance, made available on Flickr,Creative Commons Attribution 2.0 Generic (CC BY 2.0) http//commons.wikimedia.org/wiki/FileAutumn_red_peach.jpg

Pages 12-13 This work is a derivative of "Pots and Pans" is copyright © 2012 jeeheon made available on Flickr under Creative Commons Attribution 2.0 Generic (CC BY 2.0) http://www.flickr.com/photos/jeeheon/7877017204

Pages 20-21 - This work is a derivative of "Kitchen Tools at the Table" is copyright © 2012, slightly everything, Kate Hiscock, made available on Flickr under Creative Commons Attribution 2.0 Generic (CC BY 2.0) http://www.flickr.com/photos/slightlyeverything/8229722025

Pages 28-29 - This work is a derivative of "a trio of Jerry Slater cocktails" is copyright © 2007 ©2008 Southern Foodways Alliance, made available on Flickr,Creative Commons Attribution 2.0 Generic (CC BY 2.0) http://www.flickr.com/photos/southernfoodwaysalliance/2652550037/

www.ingramcontent.com/pod-product-compliance
Lightning Source LLC
Chambersburg PA
CBHW062120080426
42734CB00012B/2936